iPHONE 11 SERIES USER GUIDE

The Ultimate Guide with Tips & Tricks to Master your iPhone 11, 11 Pro and 11 Pro Max

ANTHONY BRANHAM

Goodwater Publishing
279 Stoney Lane
Dallas, TX 75212
Texas
USA

TABLE OF CONTENTS

INTRODUCTION

The iPhone 11, 11 Pro, and 11 Pro Max are Apple's latest devices released on September 20, 2019. The new iPhones have a host of new features centered on a new triple-lens camera system, and more efficient performance through the latest A13 Bionic chip and some key software optimizations.

iPhone 11

Although the iPhone 11 looks almost identical to last year's iPhone XR in size and shape, it's got two bigger and better camera. The camera has wide and ultra-wide lenses, and this feature gives users the ability to adjust cropping and zooming after the photo is taken. It also comes with a new night mode that comes on automatically to brighten pictures in low-light situations and reduces noise. It also has a next-generation Smart HDR.

QuickTake is also a new video feature that comes with the new iPhone 11. It makes it easier for you to take videos by long-pressing on the camera button. Video quality is 4K quality at 60 FPS, as well as slo-mo, and expanded dynamic range. The front-facing camera has been upgraded to 12 MP with wide-angle selfie support when the phone is in landscape. You can also take 4K video at 60 fps, as well as Slow-Mo videos.

The new iPhone 11 is available in six colors: white, black, red, purple, yellow, and green. It also features a more durable and new anodized aluminum finish. The speakers are unique and offer spatial audio, which will precisely place 5.1 surround or Dolby Atmos sound to precisely match any video that supports it.

It's powered by the new A13 Bionic chip, which Apple flaunts as its faster processor ever. The battery life of the iPhone 11 lasts one hour longer battery life than the iPhone XS. It comes with a

Lightning port, not USB-C, and still includes a 5-watt USB-A charger, not the heavier 18-watt USB-PD charger now included with the iPhone 11 Pro and Pro Max.

iPhone 11 Pro and iPhone 11 Pro Max

The iPhone 11 Pro and iPhone 11 Pro Max has the same features, and both look alike except that they differ in sizes and weight. They've got three cameras on the back now instead of two, and a giant, glossy back camera bump to go with them. It has a triple-lens 12MP rear camera array on both the iPhone 11 Pro and iPhone Pro Max. There is one f/2.4 ultra-wide lens with a 120 degree field of view and 2x optical zoom out, one f/1.8 wide lens, and one f/2.0 telephoto camera with 2x optical zoom in. All you have to do is zoom out to see more and take wider shots, from 0.5x to 2x and there is also a new Night mode to take illuminated low-light photos.

The new iPhone 11 Pro and iPhone 11 Pro Max have a Lightning port, but the cable in the box now ends with USB-C and comes with a new, 18-watt adapter that fast-charge to 50% in just 30 minutes. It's confirmed that the batteries on the iPhone 11 Pro and iPhone 11 Pro Max last 4 and 5 hours longer than last year's iPhone XS and XS Max.

They are available in gold, silver, Space Gray, and Midnight Green, a new color previously not available on iPhones.

The iPhone 11 Pro and Pro Max have an A13 Bionic processor; they also have three internal storage options: 64 GB, 256 GB, and 512 GB, and have 4 GB of RAM.

Differences between iPhone 11, iPhone 11 Pro and iPhone 11 Pro Max

Specs	iPhone 11	iPhone 11 Pro	iPhone 11 Pro Max
Types	Smartphone	Smartphone	Phablet
Operating system	iOS 13.1.2	iOS 13.1.2	iOS 13.1.2
Design	Glass and aluminum design	Textured matte glass and stainless steel design	Textured matte glass and stainless steel design
Size	150.9 x 75.7 x 8.3 mm (5.94 x 2.98 x 0.33 in)	144.0 x 71.4 x 8.1 mm (5.67 x 2.81 x 0.32 in)	158.0 x 77.8 x 8.1 mm (6.22 x 3.06 x 0.32 in)

Weight (Grams)	194g	188g	226g
Colors	Purple, Yellow, Green, Black, White, Red	Gold, Silver, Dark Gray, Midnight Green	Gold, Silver, Dark Gray, Midnight Green
Screen Display	6.1-inch LCD, Liquid Retina HD	5.8-inch OLED, Super Retina XDR	6.5-inch OLED, Super Retina XDR
Resolution	1792 x 828 pixels	2436 × 1125 pixels	2688 x 1242 pixels
Camera	Dual 12-megapixel wide and ultra-wide cameras with night mode.	Triple 12-megapixel wide, ultra-wide and telephoto cameras with night mode.	Triple 12-megapixel wide, ultra-wide and telephoto cameras with night mode.
Video	4K video recording at 24 fps, 30 fps, or 60 fps	4K video recording at 24 fps, 30 fps, or 60 fps	4K video recording at 24 fps, 30 fps, or 60 fps
Biometrics	wide-angle Face ID	wide-angle Face ID	wide-angle Face ID

Processor	Apple A13 Bionic	Apple A13 Bionic	Apple A13 Bionic
RAM	4GB	4GB	4GB
Storage	64, 128 or 256 GB	64, 256 or 512 GB	64, 256 or 512 GB
Battery	3110 mAh	3046 mAh	3969 mAh
Battery life	Video playback: Up to 17 hours; Video playback (streamed): Up to 10 hours; Audio playback: Up to 65 hours	Video playback: Up to 18 hours; Video playback (streamed): Up to 11 hours; Audio playback: Up to 65 hours	Video playback: Up to 20 hours; Video playback (streamed): Up to 12 hours; Audio playback: Up to 80 hours
Charging	Slow (5W USB Power Adapter with Lightning to USB Cable) Wireless charging	Fast (18W USB-C Power Adapter with USB-C to Lightning Cable) Wireless	Fast (18W USB-C Power Adapter with USB-C to Lightning Cable) Wireless

	support	charging support	charging support
Special features	Water and dust resistant (IP68) Dual-SIM capabilities (nano-SIM and e-SIM)	Water and dust resistant (IP68) Dual-SIM capabilities (nano-SIM and e-SIM)	Water and dust resistant (IP68) Dual-SIM capabilities (nano-SIM and e-SIM)

TOP COMMON FEATURES OF THE IPHONE 11, IPHONE 11 PRO AND IPHONE PRO MAX

Improved battery life

Last year's iPhones once boasted the best battery life of any iPhone ever released. Unfortunately, the new iPhone 11, iPhone 11 Pro, and iPhone Pro Max feature an additional hour of rated battery life compared to their predecessors. iPhone Pro Max now has the most extended battery life in an iPhone.

Spatial audio

The iPhone 11, iPhone 11 Pro and iPhone Pro Max come with an added support for spatial audio, a virtual surround decoder, which brings simulated surround to the iPhone. Dolby Atmos, 5.1 and 7.1 surround sound is supported, of which the previous iPhones lacked such support.

Repositioned Apple logo

The Apple logo on the back of the iPhone, for the first time, is repositioned to the center of the device instead of on the top half of the device.

The reason for this may probably be to add beauty to the new iPhones. Since the new rectangular camera module takes up so much space compared to previous camera designs, having an Apple logo closer to the module would have made the iPhone 11, iPhone 11 Pro and iPhone Pro Max look a bit top-heavy.

No "iPhone" text imprinted

The **iPhone** text, which generally occupies the lower half of Apple's smartphones, has been outright removed on the iPhone 11, iPhone 11 Pro and iPhone Pro Max. This, like the repositioned Apple logo, may likely have somewhat to do with visual balance. With no Apple logo on the top half of the device, having the iPhone text on the lower half of the handset would have looked odd.

Hence, Apple decided to get rid of the text altogether.

A13 Bionic CPU

The inclusion of the Apple's new A13 Bionic CPU is one of the things that gave the iPhone 11, iPhone 11 Pro and iPhone 11 Pro Max such a great value. It's confirmed that the 64-bit A13 Bionic is the fastest CPU in a smartphone as it has two **performance cores** and four **high-efficiency cores** along with an Apple-designed graphics processing unit (GPU). Despite the boost in speed, the A13 Bionic is more efficient, requiring up to 30% less power on its performance cores, up to 40% less power on its efficiency cores, and up to 40% less power from the GPU. The A13 Bionic can also utilize real-time machine learning to help optimize photos by reducing noise, enhancing colors, or adjusting the lighting on a person's face.

U1 Ultra Wideband chip

Apple's U1 Ultra Wideband chip appears for the first time in the iPhone 11, iPhone 11 Pro and iPhone 11 Pro Max bringing Ultra Wideband technology to the iPhone for the first time. The

U1 chip allows for spatial awareness, which gives the iPhone the ability to understand its precise location in relation to other U1-enabled Apple devices. In other words, this feature helps iPhones find other iPhones more precisely when they are nearby. This new technology improves the AirDrop functionality to share files faster between two iPhone 11 series devices.

Haptic Touch

The iPhone 11, iPhone 11 Pro and iPhone 11 Pro Max ditch 3D Touch for Haptic Touch. Haptic Touch works relatively the same way, except instead of having to press down harder on the screen, you'll need to merely long-press on the item. It doesn't rely on the amount of pressure applied. Haptic Touch lets you do things faster, like take selfies without launching the Camera app by pressing against the screen to access additional menu options.

Networking enhancements

The iPhone 11, iPhone 11 Pro and iPhone Pro Max feature an upgrade to Gigabit-class LTE, along with support for the Wi-Fi 6. Wi-Fi 6 is better than the previous Wi-Fi 5 as it supports faster download speeds; lets devices send more information with each transmission; lets routers and other access points service more devices at once; and facilitates better, faster performance in dense, crowded environments like airports and stadia.

Enhanced water resistance

The iPhone 11, iPhone 11 Pro and iPhone Pro Max IP 68 water and dust resistant feature beats the previous iPhones' water-resistance of up to 1 meter for up to 30 minutes depth capabilities. iPhone 11 has up to 30 minutes of water resistance for up to 2 meters depth, while both iPhone 11 Pro and iPhone 11 Pro Max is water-resistant to a depth of 4 meters for up to 30 minutes. That still doesn't mean that you should intentionally submerge your iPhone in water, but it means that you should be okay if such an accident were to occur.

Deep Fusion

Deep Fusion is a new computational photography process specifically on the iPhone 11, iPhone 11 Pro, and iPhone 11 Pro Max because of the A13 chip. It blends multiple exposures at the pixel level to create a photograph with an even higher level of detail than standard HDR.

Unlike Night mode, which has an indicator on-screen and can be turned off, Deep Fusion is invisible to the user. There's no indicator in the camera app or the photo roll. But in the background, Deep Fusion is doing quite a lot of work and operating much differently than Smart HDR. Here's the basic breakdown of how it works:

- By the time you press the shutter button, the camera has already grabbed four frames at a fast shutter speed to freeze motion in the shot and four standard frames. When you press the shutter, it grabs one longer-exposure shot to capture detail.
- Those three regular shots and long-exposure shot are merged into what Apple calls a **synthetic long**. This is a significant difference from Smart HDR.
- Deep Fusion picks the short-exposure image with the most detail and merges it with the synthetic long exposure. Unlike Smart HDR, Deep Fusion combines these two frames, not more — although the synthetic long is already made of four previously-merged frames. All the component frames are also processed for noise differently than Smart HDR, in a way that's better for Deep Fusion.

- The images are run through four detail processing steps, pixel by pixel, each tailored to increasing amounts of detail — the sky and walls are in the lowest band, while skin, hair, fabrics, and so on are the highest level. This generates a series of weightings for how to blend the two images — taking detail from one and tone, color, and luminance from the other.
- The final image is generated.

Brighter True Tone flash

The True Tone flash on the iPhone 11, iPhone 11 Pro and iPhone Pro Max are now bigger and brighter, improving low light photography workflows where a flash is required.

Redesigned Camera app

The Camera app found on the iPhone 11, iPhone 11 Pro and iPhone Pro Max have been completely rebuilt with brand new design, intuitive controls, and tons of new changes and features. You'll also notice a new font, created explicitly for the new Camera app UI, which further complements the new digs. The most significant difference between the prior iOS Camera app and the one featured on the new iPhone 11 series has to do with the new ultra-wide camera.

Swiping up on the viewfinder interface will reveal a new tray of options for manually managing the flash, Night Mode, Live Photos, aspect ratio, timer, and filter. Gone is the dedicate Square shooting mode now that the aspect ratio setting is available with options of the square (1:1), 4:3, and 16:9 (cropped).

Night mode

Google's **Night Sight** feature on their Pixel 3 smartphone was a big hit among Android users, and now Apple has its take on providing users with improved low light photography without the need for a harsh and unnatural-looking flash. Dubbed **Night mode**, this feature automatically kicks in when the wide or telephoto camera detects there isn't enough light in a scene. A night mode icon with a recommended exposure time (usually between 1-5 seconds) appears next to the flash icon, and when you tap the shutter button, an exposure meter counts down to indicate how long you should hold still. The meter is also used to manually turn night mode off or switch to the maximum recommended exposures.

As long as you use Night mode in ideal environments, you can come up with some awesome photos, even in areas devoid of light. It's not on the same level as a manual mirrorless camera with the ability to open the aperture and manually slow down the shutter speed, but it's a tremendous automatic feature for smartphone users that will open up photographic possibilities in new environments.

QuickTake video

When shooting photos with your iPhone 11, iPhone 11 Pro or iPhone Pro Max in normal Photo mode, you can long-press on the shutter button to initiate a video recording without switching to video mode. Once you release your finger from the shutter, the video will stop recording. If you slide your finger to the right while long-pressing the shutter button, the video will continuously record.

If you're wondering where burst mode went, tap the shutter and slide your finger to the left. Continue holding your finger down for as long as you wish to take a burst of photos.

Audio Zoom

When you zoom in when shooting videos with iPhone 11, iPhone 11 Pro or iPhone Pro Max, the microphone will focus in on your subject to create the sensation of your audio **zooming in** along with the video.

4K 60 FPS video across all cameras

For the first time in an iPhone, you can now record video in 4K resolution at up to 60 frames per second (FPS) on every camera on the iPhone 11, iPhone 11 Pro and iPhone 11 Pro Max. That includes the wide-angle camera, ultra-wide camera, and even the front-facing TrueDepth Camera.

Next-generation Smart HDR

The new iPhone 11, iPhone 11 Pro, and iPhone 11 Pro Max has an improved Smart HDR feature available for both the front and rear-facing cameras on the iPhone. You'll no longer find the option to keep a copy of the non-HDR photo when Smart HDR is enabled. The next-generation Smart HDR features a 10-bit pipeline vs. the 8-bit pipeline of the previous generation, allowing for more natural-looking skin tones, shadow roll-off, highlights, etc.

12MP TrueDepth Camera

Face ID works through a set of sensors built into the front cameras of the iPhone 11, iPhone 11 Pro or iPhone 11 Pro Max, and are called the **TrueDepth** Camera. This camera, in addition to powering Face ID with the additional biometric components, is also a standard front-facing camera that can be used to take selfies.

This TrueDepth 12-megapixel camera is capable of recording 60 FPS videos in 4K with support for extended dynamic range video at 30 fps. When using the TrueDepth camera for a selfie in a landscape mode, the result is a 12-megapixel photo while in a portrait mode, it will use a zoomed 7-megapixel photo.

Auto Zoom out

When placing the front-facing camera into landscape mode, the camera will automatically **zoom out** by removing the crop and going back to its native 23mm focal length. Of course, you can use the **zoom** button to toggle digital zoom.

The wider focal length is perfect for group selfies, which is why auto-zoom kicks in when your phone is placed in landscape mode.

Slo-mo selfies

The front-facing camera supports the slow motion at 120fps for the first time on an iPhone, which Apple has somewhat cringingly dubbed **slofies**. On older iPhone hardware, the camera would automatically switch to the rear-facing camera when switching to slo-mo mode, but on the iPhone 11, iPhone 11 Pro or iPhone 11 Pro Max, you can freely switch between the cameras while in slo-mo mode. Keep in mind that slow-motion video will always look better when using the rear-facing camera thanks to the better optics and support for 240 fps for super-smooth slow motion.

SETTING UP YOUR IPHONE 11, 11 PRO AND 11 PRO MAX

Setting up a new iPhone is an exciting experience. The moment you turn on your new iPhone for the first time, you'll be greeted with **Hello** in a variety of languages. Whether you are setting up your device as new or restoring from another iPhone or switching from an Android phone, the procedure is the same for the three models of the iPhone 11 series. Follow the steps below to set up your iPhone and please note that the procedure is the same for iPhone 11, 11 Pro and 11 Pro Max.

1. Power on your new phone. To turn it on, hold the right side button until the Apple logo appears and then release it.
2. You will be greeted with **Hello** in a variety of languages on the welcome screen.
3. Touch **slide to set up** and slide your finger across the screen to get started.
4. Choose your **language** and your location (**country** or **region**).
5. Select a **wi-fi network**. If you are not in a wi-fi network range, you can set this up later. Select **Cellular** instead.
   - At this point, you can choose to use **Automatic Setup** to set up your new iPhone with the same passcode and settings as your old iPhone. If you

decide to set up your new iPhone manually, continue with the following steps.

6. Tap **Continue** after reading about Apple's Data & Privacy information.
7. Tap **Enable Location Services**. If you don't want to enable location services at this time, select **Skip Location Services**. You can enable certain location services manually, like **Maps**.
8. Set up **Face ID**.
9. Create a **Passcode**. You can set up a standard six-digit passcode, or create a four-digit passcode or custom passcode by tapping **Passcode Options**.

At this juncture, you will be asked if you want to set up your iPhone as new, restore from an old backed-up iPhone, or move data from an Android phone.

- **Set up as new iPhone**

This means starting every setting anew, and it's for people who may have never used an iPhone before or want their iPhone to feel genuinely brand new.

- **Restore from a previous iPhone backup**

You can do this online with iCloud or over USB with iTunes. This is for people who've had a previous iPhone and are moving to a newer model.

- **Import from an Android Phone**

Apple has an app in Google Play to make switching from Android to iPhone easier. This is for people switching to iPhone.

How to set up your iPhone 11, iPhone 11 Pro, or iPhone 11 Pro Max as new

1. Set up your iPhone until you reach the screen titled **Apps & Data**.
2. Tap **Set Up as New iPhone**.
3. Enter your **Apple ID** and **password**. If you don't have one, you can create a new one by tapping **Don't have an Apple ID?** and follow the onscreen instructions to create a new one.
4. Read and **Agree** to Apple's terms and conditions.
5. Tap **Agree** again to confirm.
6. Set up **Apple Pay**.
7. Set up **iCloud Keychain**.
8. Set up **Siri** and **Hey, Siri**.
9. Tap **Send Diagnostic information to Apple** when apps crash or other issues arise, or tap **Don't Send** if you don't want to send.
10. Turn on **Display Zoom** for extra visual accessibility.
11. Tap **Get Started**.

How to restore or transfer your data from a previous iPhone

If you decide to upgrade to the latest iPhone 11, 11 Pro or 11 Pro Max from an older iPhone version or model, you'll likely want to move as much of the data from your old iPhone over to your new device as you can. There are two ways you can restore your apps and data from your old iPhone using iCloud or connecting to your computer and back it up via iTunes. Whichever one you choose, you must make sure your old iPhone is backed up first.

Backing up and restoring your data from iCloud

1. Tap **Settings** on your old iPhone.
2. Tap the **Apple ID banner**.
3. Tap **iCloud**.
4. Tap **iCloud Backup**.
5. Tap **Back Up Now**.
6. Wait for the backup to complete before proceeding.
7. Turn your old iPhone off once the backup is finished.
8. Remove the SIM card from your old iPhone or if you're going to move it to your new one.

You can now set aside your old iPhone. Make sure that your new iPhone is off when you start these next steps.

1. Insert your old SIM card into your new iPhone if you want to move it between devices.
2. Turn on your new iPhone.
3. Set up your iPhone until you reach the screen titled **Apps & Data**.
4. Tap **Restore from iCloud backup**.
5. Sign in to your **iCloud account** (This is the same as your Apple ID).
6. Tap **Next**.
7. Tap **Agree**.
8. Tap **Agree** again.
9. Choose the backup you just made.

Backing up and restoring your data using iTunes

1. Make sure you're running the most recent version of iTunes.
2. Connect your old iPhone to your Mac or Windows PC.
3. Launch **iTunes**.
4. Click on the **iPhone icon** in the menu bar when it appears.
5. Click on **Encrypt Backup**; you'll be asked to add a password if this is your first time encrypting a backup.

6. Click on **Back Up Now**.
7. Skip **Backup Apps**, if asked as they will likely be re-downloaded anyway.
8. Wait for the backup to complete before unplugging your old iPhone.
9. Take your SIM card out of your old iPhone. (If you need to use the same SIM card for your new phone.)

You can now set aside your old iPhone. Make sure that your new iPhone is off before starting these next steps.

1. Put your SIM card into your new iPhone.
2. Turn on your new iPhone.
3. Set up your iPhone until you reach the screen titled **Apps & Data**.
4. Plug your new iPhone into your Mac or Windows PC.
5. Select **Restore from iTunes backup**.
6. On **iTunes** on your Mac or Windows PC, select **Restore from this backup**.
7. Choose your recent backup from the list.
8. Click **Continue**.
9. Enter your **password** if your backup was encrypted and it asks.

Keep your iPhone plugged into iTunes until the transfer is complete and on Wi-Fi until all re-downloads are complete. Depending on how much data you have to re-download, including music and apps, it might take a while.

How to move data from an Android device

Transferring data from an Android phone to an Apple iPhone can only be possible with the use of an Apple's free app called **Move to iOS,** and it's available in the Google Play Store. This means that before you move your data to your new iPhone, you download **Move to iOS** on your Android phone. Follow the steps below to transfer your data from an Android phone to your new iPhone 11, 11 Pro or 11 Pro Max.

1. Set up your iPhone until you reach the screen titled **Apps & Data**.
2. Tap **Move Data from Android** option.
3. On your Android phone, open the **Google Play Store** and search for **Move to iOS** app.
4. Open the **Move to iOS** app listing.
5. Tap **Install**
6. Tap **Accept** to accept the permissions request.
7. Tap **Open** after it's installed.
8. Tap **Continue** on both devices.
9. Tap **Agree** and then **Next** on the Android phone.
10. On your Android device, enter the **12-digit code** displayed on the iPhone.

After entering the code, the Android device will connect with your iPhone over a peer-to-peer Wi-Fi connection.

11. It will ask whether you want to transfer your **Google Account** info (so that you can quickly login into your Google account on your new Apple device), **Bookmarks**, **Messages**, **Contacts**, **Photos** and **Videos** in your camera roll. Select everything you want to move over.

Your Android phone or tablet will transfer the selected data over to your iPhone and place the appropriate content into the correct apps. Once the transfer process is complete, tap on **Continue Setting Up iPhone** on your device and carry on setting up a new Apple ID or logging in to the accounts you transferred from your old Android device. Do that, and then you're good to go!

TIPS AND TRICKS FOR IPHONE 11, 11 PRO AND 11 PRO MAX

GET A HOME BUTTON

While the iPhone 11, 11 Pro and 11 Pro Max can't have a physical Home button, it can have a virtual Home button in the form of Assistive Touch. This can be turned on in the following way.

1. Launch **Settings** app and tap **Accessibility**.
2. Tap **Touch** and toggle **Assistive Touch** switch to **On**.

The white **Assistive Touch** button will be enabled on the screen. Tap the button to access **Home**, **Control Centre**, **Device**, **Notifications**, **Gestures**, or **Custom**.

ACTIVATE REACHABILITY MODE

Unlike the other gestures, you do need to set it up first.

1. Launch **Settings** app.
2. Tap on **Accessibility**.
3. Tap on **Touch**.
4. Toggle **Reachability** switch to **On**.

Once set up:

1. Touch your finger to the gesture area at the very bottom of the iPhone 11 or 11 Pro display.
2. Swipe down.

CUSTOMIZE HAPTIC TOUCH

How long it will take Haptic Touch to respond depends on whether it's set at fast or slow. To customize this, follow the steps below.

1. Launch **Settings** app.
2. Tap on **Accessibility**.
3. Tap on **Touch**.
4. Select to tick either **Slow** or **Fast**.

SET UP FACE ID

Face ID is Apple's name for the biometric facial identity scanner on its latest iPhone devices. You can authenticate Apple Pay, iTunes & App store transactions and Password Auto fill. But you have to set it up first!

Setting up Face ID is similar to setting up Touch ID, only more accessible. iOS will offer to let you set up Face ID as part of your initial iPhone setup. But you can also set up Face ID – and reset it – anytime.

1. Launch **Settings** and tap **Face ID & Passcode**.
2. Enter your **Passcode**.
3. Tap **Set Up Face ID**.
4. Tap **Get Started**.
5. As the scan circles appear, scan your face by rotating it in a circular motion while keeping your eyes focused on the camera. Once the grey ticks around the circle have all turned green, you can proceed to the next step.
6. Tap **Continue**.
7. Re-scan your face again by rotating your face while still looking at the camera again.
8. Tap **Done**.

Now you can start using Face ID on your new iPhone but make sure Face ID is enabled for unlocking your device. To enable it, do the following.

At the top of the **Face ID & Passcode** page, tap the **iPhone Unlock** switch if it's white, thus this will cause the switch to turn green, thus indicating that Face ID can now be used to unlock your device.

Turning Off Require Attention for Face ID

By default, your iPhone 11, iPhone 11 Pro and iPhone 11 Pro Max devices will require you look at it before it authenticates. If you want to be able to unlock it without looking directly at your iPhone screen, for accessibility or convenience reasons, you can turn it off. Although this method is not as secure, it still has to see your eyes, nose, and mouth to authenticate you.

1. Launch **Settings** and tap **Face ID & Passcode**.
2. Enter your **Passcode**.
3. Toggle **Require Attention for Face ID** to **Off**.
4. Tap **Ok** on the security warning.

Turning On Require Attention for Face ID

If you want to turn attention mod back **On** for a Face ID in an iPhone 11, iPhone 11 Pro or iPhone 11 Pro Max to enjoy auto-expanding notifications, auto-muffling alarms, and enhanced security. Here's how.

1. Launch **Settings** and tap **Face ID & Passcode**.
2. Enter your **Passcode**.
3. Toggle **Require Attention for Face ID** to **On**.

4. Toggle **Attention Aware Features** to **On**.

Resetting your Face ID

If you want to switch the person's face that's registered on your iPhone or, for whatever reason, you want to redo your Face ID setup, the steps below will help you. Please note that there is no confirmation in this procedure so the moment you tap the button, your Face ID will be gone and you will have to set it up again to get it back.

1. Launch **Settings** and tap **Face ID & Passcode**.
2. Enter your **Passcode**.
3. Tap Reset **Face ID**.

SET UP TWO FACE IDS

Two different Face IDs can be set up on the new iPhone 11 series with the second one serving as an alternative in case of emergency. Follow the steps below to set up the second face as an **Alternate Appearance**.

1. Launch **Settings** and tap **Face ID & Passcode**.
2. Tap **Set Up Alternate Appearance**.

3. Tap **Get Started** and follow the on-screen instruction to register the new face.

TURN ON OPTIMIZED BATTERY CHARGING

The new iOS 13.1.1 that comes with your iPhone 11, iPhone 11 Pro or iPhone Pro Max has an **Optimized Battery Charging** feature. This feature is intended to help prolong your battery's life by learning your charging habits and preventing the battery from immediately charging to 100%. It learns your nightly charging habits, using any set alarms in the **Clock** app, to properly charge your iPhone's battery each night and reduce the amount it degrades over time. If you usually charge overnight while you sleep, Optimized Battery Charging will keep your iPhone's battery at 80% for most of the night, finishing off the last 20% of charge right before your alarm goes off. The result is a healthier charging cycle for your phone's battery and a battery that will last longer. To turn on **Battery Optimization Charging** in the iPhone 11, iPhone 11 Pro or iPhone Pro Max, follow the steps below.

1. Launch **Settings** and tap **Battery**.
2. Tap **Battery Health** and toggle **Optimized Battery Charging to On**.

CHECK BATTERY STATUS

To check the battery status of your iPhone 11, 11 Pro or Pro Max, follow the steps below.

1. Launch **Settings** and tap **Battery**.
2. Tap **Battery Health** and select **Maximum Capacity** in percentage.

FORCE QUIT (KILL) APPS

It's so easy. You can force quit all the things with just a simple swipe as thus.

1. Touch your finger to the gesture area at the very bottom of the iPhone 11 display.
2. Swipe up slightly.
3. Pause. Don't lift your finger immediately. (That'll take you Home.) Just. Pause.
4. Lift your finger.
5. Swipe up on an app card. Poof! It's gone.

Once you're in a killing mode, you can kill as many apps as you want. Just remember, iOS prefers to manage apps for you, so only kill them if they deserve to die.

TAKE AN ULTRA-WIDE PHOTO

The new iPhone 11, iPhone 11 Pro and iPhone 11 Pro Max have wide, ultra-wide and telephoto cameras at the back for capturing photos and videos with a 120-degree field-of-view. That means you can zoom out to capture more of your surroundings in a shot.

Shooting with your iPhone 11 series entails switching between Ultra-Wide, Wide, and Telephoto cameras depending on what you want. On opening the **Camera** app, you can choose between the different lenses by tapping the numbered buttons at the bottom of the viewfinder: **0.5x** is the new ultra-wide lens, **1x** is the standard wide lens, and **2** is the telephoto lens (iPhone 11 Pro and Pro Max only).

TAKE A SLOFIE

The front-facing camera on the iPhone 11 has a few new tricks, including the ability to capture a slofie. That's Apple's name for a 120 frame-per-second slow-motion selfie. The slofie can be taken in the following ways.

1. Launch the **Camera** app.
2. Tap the **Perspective Flip** button to activate the front-facing camera.
3. Swipe the **Mode Dial** to the right until you're on **Slo-Mo** mode.

4. Take your **Slofie** by tapping on the **shutter** button, then move around really fast or jump up and down.

TAKE A QUICK VIDEO

1. Open **Camera** app on your iPhone.
2. Tap and hold on the **shutter** button with the camera in Photo mode. Your video recording will now begin, and lifting your finger at this point will cause the video recording to stop.
3. Swipe the **recording** button to the **lock** icon on the right. This will keep your recording going even when you lift your finger from your iPhone.

TAKE BURST PHOTOS

Burst Mode refers to when the camera on your iPhone captures a series of photos in rapid succession, at a rate of ten frames per second. It's a great way to shoot an action scene or an unexpected event since you're always more likely to end up with the picture you were aiming for.

1. Launch **Camera** app on your iPhone.
2. Press the **shutter** button and drag it towards the square displaying the last image you shot.

This has to be done quickly, so you don't start a quick video recording.

3. Lift your finger from the **shutter** button to stop taking your burst photo.

When you take a series of burst photos, they automatically appear in the **Photos** app under the Album name **Bursts**.

ACTIVATE DARK MODE

To activate Dark Mode, you need to do the following to activate it.

1. Launch **Settings** app.
2. Tap on **Display & Brightness**.
3. Select **Dark** to activate it.

TAKE A NIGHT MODE PHOTO

The new iPhone 11, 11 Pro and 11 Pro Max has a new Night Mode explicitly designed for taking photos in low-light environments of below 10 lux. Your iPhone will automatically detect when Night Mode is necessary based on the amount of light it detects and suggests enabling it by showing a small icon that looks like a crescent moon with a couple of lines through it. Tap that icon to turn on Night Mode, and it will turn yellow. Next to the icon will be a time, such as "1s" or "5s." That's how long in seconds your iPhone 11 requires to take the Night Mode photo and capture all of the information and light necessary to produce a great-looking shot.

Tap on the **shutter** button when you're ready to take the photo and try to hold the phone steady until the shutter button is active again. Moving around while a Night Mode photo is captured can lead to blurry shots.

RECORD VIDEO WHILE TAKING A PHOTO (QUICKTAKE)

QuickTake is a new feature on the latest iPhone 11, 11 Pro and 11 Pro Max that lets you easily capture video without switching between modes. Hold down the shutter button or volume button while using the Photo mode of the Camera app, then capture video until you release the button. You can even slide the on-screen shutter button over to lock in video mode on the spot.

QuickTake works on the entire front and rear cameras. One thing to be mindful of is the aspect ratio. If your photos are set to 4:3, QuickTake videos will also be that aspect ratio. For 16:9 videos, you'll need to set the photo aspect ratio accordingly.

SELECT CAMERA ASPECT RATIO

The redesigned **Camera** app in the iPhone 11, iPhone 11 Pro and iPhone 11 Pro Max made provision for the introduction of different aspect ratio shooting modes. Unlike the earlier iPhone's **Camera** app which has only 1:1 aspect ratio, the users of the iPhone 11, iPhone 11 Pro, and iPhone 11 Pro Max can choose between three aspect ratio options when shooting in the Camera app: 1:1, 4:3, and 16:9. To get to the different shooting modes, follow these steps.

1. Launch the **Camera** app, then tap the chevron at the top of the viewfinder (or to the side of it, if you're shooting in landscape) to reveal the hidden drawer.
2. Tap the **4:3** button in the toolset that appears directly below (or to the side of) the viewfinder.
3. Select your preferred aspect ratio from the expanded 4:3 button menu.
4. Proceed to take your shot.
5. Note that the 1:1 and 16:9 ratios are non-destructive. In other words, you can re-crop them in the editing window if you later decide you want to return to the typical 4:3 frame.

ACTIVATE SCREEN RECORD

This feature allows you to record or keep tracks of every activity going on the screen of your new iPhone series. First you must add it to the **Control Centre**. To do so, follow the steps below.

1. Launch **Settings** app.
2. Tap on **Control Centre**.
3. Tap on **Customize Control** and select **Screen Recording** to add it to the Control Centre.

   From the Control Centre, you can activate the Screen Record.

To stop the Screen Recording

Press the red recording bar to stop the recording; a confirmation screen will appear to either **Cancel** the deactivation or **Stop** the Screen Recording. This will automatically save the **Screen Recording** videos to **Photos**.

To record the video together with the audio around your iPhone series while Screen Recording, follow the steps below.

1. Go to **Control Centre** by swiping from top to bottom.
2. Long press the **Screen Recording** icon.
3. Select **Turn the Microphone On**.

TAKE A SCREENSHOT

The following ways will help you to screen in your new device by using the Side button since there is no physical Home button.

1. Open the app or screen you want to capture.

2. Set up everything exactly the way you want it for the shot.
3. Press and hold the **Side** button on the right side of your iPhone 11, 11 Pro or 11 Pro Max.
4. Click the **Volume Up** button at the same time.
5. The screen will flash white, and you'll hear the camera shutter sound (if your sound is enabled).

TURN ON TEXT, CALL, AND FACETIME FORWARDING

This feature is vital if you have other Apple devices such as Apple Watch or iPad and may wish to text, call, or use FaceTime from there. This won't work with Apple TV as it's not equipped for calls or messaging of any kind. To activate these features, do the following.

For calls: launch **Settings** app and tap **Phone**, then select **Calls on Other Devices** for the devices you'd like to receive calls on and toggle the switch **On**.

For messages: launch **Settings** app and tap **Messages**, then select **Text Message Forwarding** for the devices you'd like to receive calls on and toggle the switch **On**.

For FaceTime: launch **Settings** app and tap **FaceTime**. Make sure your phone number or the Apple ID you're using on both devices is selected under **You Can Be Reached By FaceTime At**.

TURN OFF THE TWO-MINUTE EXPIRATION TIME ON AUDIO MESSAGES

Most iMessages are being treated by Apple's iPhone as a sort of Snapchat-like **Listen once then it's gone forever** message. This is because, by default, iPhone 11, 11 Pro and Pro Max have an expiration period of two minutes, and the only other option is **Never**. If you need to cancel the default, follow the steps below.

1. Launch **Settings** app and tap **Messages**.
2. Tap **Audio Messages** and tap **Expire** and select **Never**.

IDENTIFY NON-GENUINE DISPLAYS AND SHOW AN ALERT

The new iPhone 11, iPhone 11 Pro, and iPhone 11 Pro Max has a feature to display an on-screen warning (shown below) if the devices are unable to verify a genuine display after a screen repair job. Apple said that non-certified displays might have some issues, including degraded multi-touch performance, unintentional touches, incorrect color calibration, and even more battery drain. They also said that notification would appear on the affected iPhone's lock screen for four days after a problem is first detected. Then it would move to the main settings menu for fifteen more days. After that, it can only be seen if you do the following.

- Launch **Settings** and tap **General**, then select **About**.

Important Display Message

Unable to verify this iPhone has a genuine Apple display.

Learn More

FORCE RESTART

You'll need to perform the following steps in quick succession to force restart iPhone 11, iPhone 11 Pro, iPhone 11 or Pro Max.

1. Quickly press and release the **Volume Up** button.

2. Quickly press and release the **Volume Down** button.
3. Press and hold the **Side** button until the Apple logo appears, then release the **Side** button.

During this process, you will see a slider to power off the iPhone. You're going to want to ignore it and continue holding down the Side button until the screen goes black. At that point, the Apple logo will pop up, and after the restart is complete, the screen will activate once again.

ENTER DFU MODE

If you are using Apple iPhone for the first time, the question that may arise is **what is DFU mode?** DFU is an acronym for **Device Firmware Update mode** and this feature could prove a handy solution when no other trick is working. It could help you to reset your iPhone fully and install a new software update. It's a useful troubleshooting method if things do go awry. It allows the device to be restored from any state. In the DFU mode, you can download firmware if required as it skips the **iBoot** boot loader.

However, entering the DFU Mode requires a bit of expertise as you need to press and hold different buttons for a specific period. If you don't succeed in the first attempt, then you should try again.

To enter the DFU mode, you will need the following things – your iPhone, a computer, and a Lightning cable. Now, let's look at the steps of how to enter DFU Mode on the iPhone 11, iPhone 11 Pro, or iPhone 11 Max.

1. Connect your iPhone to your computer and make sure that iTunes is running.
2. Turn your iPhone off if it is powered on.
3. Quickly Press and Release the **Volume Up** button.
4. Quickly press and release the Volume Down button.
5. Press and hold the **Side** button until the screen turns black.
6. After the screen turns black, continue holding the **Side** button and simultaneously hold the **Volume Down** button. Hold both of them for 5 seconds and release the **Side** Button but continue holding the **Volume Down** button for another 10 seconds. (If done correctly then the screen should remain black, it might take a few attempts to get to it.)
7. Once the screen remains black with no logos or text, then launch iTunes on your Mac or PC. A message saying **iTunes has detected an iPhone in recovery**

mode. You must restore this iPhone before it can be used with iTunes, will pop-up. After this pop-up, you will enter the DFU mode, and you will get the option to restore your iPhone.

And now you're done. Your iPhone is in DFU mode, and you can update it using iTunes. Just follow the steps on-screen. Please note that DFU is an essential feature for iPhones, but it should be used only as a last resort or in dire circumstances because it deletes all your data.

How to exit DFU mode

Once you have restored your device or made necessary changes in it, you would need to follow these simple steps to exit the black screen DFU mode

1. Quickly press and release the **Volume Up** button.
2. Quickly press and release the **Volume Down** button.
3. Press and hold the **Side** button until you see the Apple logo appears.